The
Statue of Liberty

Debra Hess

BENCHMARK BOOKS

MARSHALL CAVENDISH
NEW YORK

Benchmark Books
Marshall Cavendish
99 White Plains Road
Tarrytown, NY 10591-9001
www.marshallcavendish.com

Library of Congress Cataloging-in-Publication Data
Hess, Debra.
  The Statue of Liberty / by Debra Hess.
      p. cm. — (Symbols of America)
Summary: Traces the origins of the Statue of Liberty, its creators, the
different symbols and their meanings, and what it stands for today.
Includes bibliographical references and index.
  ISBN 0-7614-1707-9
  1. Statue of Liberty (New York, N.Y.) —Juvenile literature. 2.
New York (N.Y.) —Buildings, structures, etc. —Juvenile literature.
[1. Statue of Liberty (New York, N.Y.) 2. New York (N.Y.) —Buildings,
structures, etc.] I. Title. II. Series: Hess, Debra.   Symbols of America.

  F128.64.L6H47 2003
  974.7'1—dc21

                              2003004272

Photo Research by Anne Burns Images

Cover Photo by: Photri

Photri: 1, 7, 23, 27, 31, 35. *National Park Service*: 4,20,24,28. *Northwind*: 8, 16, 19.
Granger Collection: 11, 12, 15. *Superstock*: 32. *Getty Images*: Ray Stubblebine: 36.

Series design by Adam Mietlowski

Printed in Italy

1 3 5 6 4 2

Contents

CHAPTER ONE

Lady Liberty

In the middle of New York Harbor a statue stands as tall as a building. It is a statue of a lady wearing a crown upon her head and raising her right arm toward the sky. In her hand is a torch. While there is no real fire, the torch stands for the *eternal* flame of freedom. In her left hand she holds a *tablet* bearing the date, July 4, 1776. This is the day the United States *proclaimed* its independence from England. The lady welcomes new Americans to a land where they can be free. Her name is Liberty Enlightening the World, but everyone calls her the Statue of Liberty. Liberty means freedom.

◄ *The Statue of Liberty was designed by Frenchman Gustave Eiffel—the same man who designed the Eiffel Tower in Paris, France.*

5

The Statue of Liberty is one of the most famous American symbols in the world. She is more than one hundred years old. The statue, which is 305 feet (93 meters) tall—including the *pedestal*—was given to the United States as a gift by France in 1886. The French wanted to celebrate the friendship that began between the two countries after the American Revolution. The American Revolution is the war the thirteen British colonies fought to get independence from England and to form the United States of America. France helped the colonists win the war, and thousands of

Did You Know?

- The Statue of Liberty stands 151 feet (34 meters) tall from her heel to the top of her head. The pedestal is 154 feet (47 meters) high.
- Her nose is 4 feet 6 inches (1.37 meters) long.
- Her index finger is 8 feet (2.4 meters) long.
- Her head is 10 feet (3 meters) from ear to ear.
- Her mouth is 3 feet (1 meter) wide.
- Her waist is 35 feet (11 meters) thick.

A view from the bottom. The Statue of Liberty measures just over 305 feet (93 meters) from the ground to the tip of the torch.

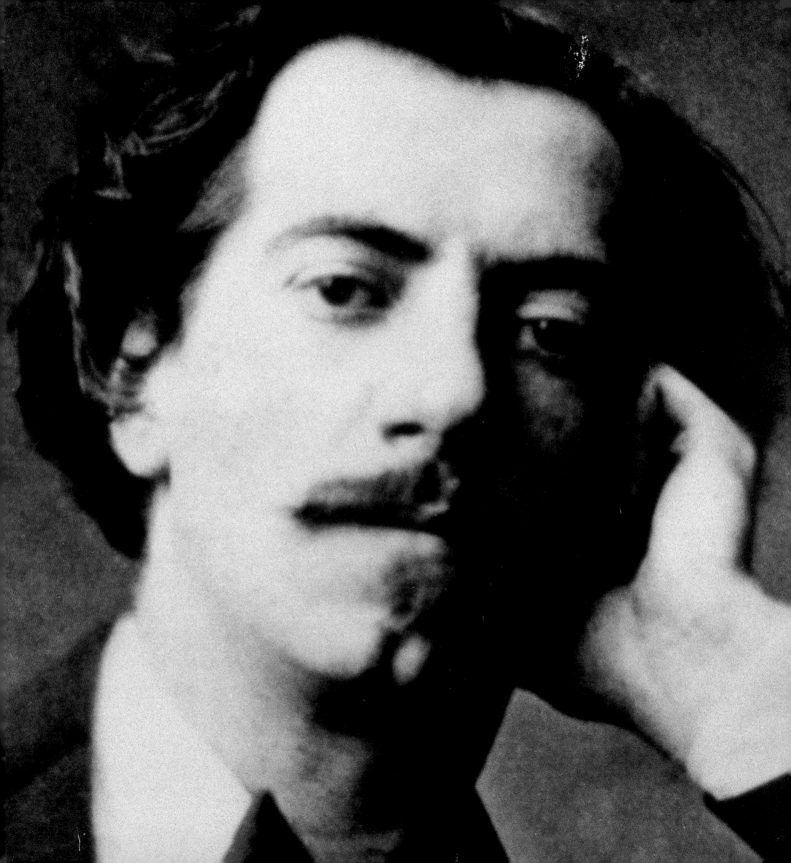

French people fought alongside Americans in that war. The success of the American Revolution *inspired* the French when they fought their own revolution in 1789 against a cruel king. Their battle cry was "Liberty, Equality, Fraternity!"

Almost one hundred years later, on a warm summer evening in 1865, a Frenchman named Édouard de Laboulaye had a dinner party at his home in Versailles, France. Laboulaye had written several well-known books about the United States. Over dinner, everyone started talking about the friendship between America and France. It was then that Laboulaye came up with the idea of giving America a present to celebrate the nation's hundredth birthday. After many more dinners and meetings, the idea of the Statue of Liberty was born. One of the guests at these dinners and meetings was a famous French *sculptor* named Frédéric-Auguste Bartholdi. He liked the idea and agreed that if the money could be raised, he would build the statue. In the end, the people of France raised $250,000 to pay for their present to America.

Frédéric-Auguste Bartholdi, the sculptor of the Statue of Liberty

CHAPTER TWO

Symbols of Freedom

It took many people to create and build the famous lady. Frenchman Alexandre-Gustave Eiffel built the inside of the statue.

The outer "skin" was made of several hundred copper sheets that were hammered against a full-size wooden frame of the statue. The sheets were then fastened together with bolts. The skin was only about as thick as a penny so it needed strong support. Eiffel built an iron skeleton for the inside of the statue. Then he and his workers spent almost a year attaching the copper skin, designed by Bartholdi.

The Statue of Liberty being built in Paris, France. Its sculptor, Frédéric-Auguste Bartholdi, stands at the right corner. ▶

This skeleton had a central tower with many iron bars *extending* from it. At the end of each bar was an iron "rib" that fit into copper brackets on the inside of the copper skin. Liberty Enlightening the World was completed in France in 1884. When it was finished, it stood in a *courtyard* outside Bartholdi's workshop. It stood there for a long time because the Americans had not yet begun working on the statue's pedestal.

The Statue of Liberty rises from Bartholdi's courtyard, looming over the streets of Paris.

Did You Know?

- Total weight of copper in the statue: 62,000 pounds (28,123 kilograms).
- Total weight of steel in the statue: 250,000 pounds (113,398 kilograms).
- Total weight of the foundation: 54 million pounds (24.5 million kilograms).

13

American architect Richard Morris Hunt designed the concrete and granite pedestal. Engineer Charles P. Stone was in charge of building it. Construction began in August 1884, a month after the statue had been completed in Paris. But before the base was even half finished, money ran out and work stopped. Many Americans did not understand that Lady Liberty was a present to all American people. They thought she was to be a lighthouse for New York City. They did not want to raise money for it. They thought only New Yorkers should pay.

In 1886, an American newspaper published this engraving of the pedestal. ▶

A newspaper owner named Joseph Pulitzer decided to use his paper, the New York *World*, to help. He wrote articles asking people for money to build the pedestal. He promised to print in his paper the name of every single person who sent money. The money came pouring in. Some people sent less than one dollar. But it was enough. By August 1885, Pulitzer had raised $100,000. The pedestal was finally finished in 1886.

◀ *An illustration of Joseph Pulitzer holding a printing press.*

In May 1885, the Statue of Liberty was shipped to the United States in 350 pieces that were packed in 214 crates. It took four months to reassemble the statue on the pedestal. The French had wanted to give the statue to America in time for the hundredth anniversary of the signing of the Declaration of Independence in 1776. On October 28, 1886, the Statue of Liberty was dedicated in New York in front of 4,000 people. President Grover Cleveland accepted the statue on behalf of the American people. She was a birthday present that was ten years late!

The dedication celebration of the Statue of Liberty in May 1885 ▶

When you look at pictures of the Statue of Liberty or visit her in person, you might notice several symbols that Bartholdi worked into his design.

The torch, for example, was the first part of the statue to be built. It symbolizes the light that is the key to freedom. The torch was taken down in 1984 because of damage and was replaced with a new flame in 1986. The new flame is made of copper that has been dipped in gold. The torch has never had a real flame.

In 50-mile-per-hour winds, the torch can sway up to 5 inches (12.7 cm).

Did You Know?

- Visitors must climb 354 steps (equal to 22 stories) to reach the crown.
- Lady Liberty stands on 58 acres (24 hectares) of land named Liberty Island in the middle of New York Harbor.
- When wind speeds reach 50 miles (80 kilometers) per hour, the statue sways 3 inches (7.62 centimeters) in either direction.

21

The Statue of Liberty wears a crown with seven spikes. Bartholdi chose seven spikes to symbolize that liberty should spread across the seven seas and the seven continents of the world. There are twenty-five windows in the crown, representing the earth's gemstones.

Lady Liberty is dressed in a free-flowing robe called a *stola*. Over the stola, she is wearing a cloak called a *palla*, which is fastened by a clasp on her left shoulder. The Roman goddess Libertas wore such an outfit. She was the goddess worshipped by freed slaves.

If the Statue of Liberty were wearing a real cloak, it would be made of 4,000 square yards (1,100 square meters) of fabric!

Sandals are also an important symbol in the statue's design. Lady Liberty wears sandals, which symbolizes that she is free to walk the earth as she pleases. Even though she is on a pedestal, Lady Liberty is actually walking forward. She is lighting the path to freedom through peace.

And finally, broken chains lie at Lady Liberty's feet. They symbolize that the statue is free from slavery.

Lady Liberty wears a size 879 women's shoe!

CHAPTER THREE
Ellis Island

Not far from the Statue of Liberty in New York Harbor is Ellis Island. From 1892 to 1954, Ellis Island was the main port of entry for millions of immigrants into the United States. Today over 100 million Americans can trace their roots to relatives who came to the United States through Ellis Island. The first immigrants came on steamships from across the Atlantic Ocean.

Did anyone in your family come to the United States through Ellis Island?

Most passengers traveled in steerage—the lower parts of a ship. Ships carried anywhere from a few hundred to more than 2,000 steerage passengers. They spent their days in filthy, windowless rooms, rocked by the waves of the ocean, with little water and even less food. They were not allowed to go to the upper parts of the ships.

◄ *Overcrowding was a problem on steamships to Ellis Island.*

The journey was hard, and many people died before they ever reached America. When they did reach shore, they had to be checked by a doctor. If they were sick or had any physical problems, they were given treatment at a special hospital on Ellis Island. Then they were allowed to enter the country. A few were not admitted, but most were. When the newly arrived immigrants finally left Ellis Island, the first thing they saw was Lady Liberty, her torch held high, lighting the way to freedom.

These newly arrived immigrants were given a quick physical exam. ▶

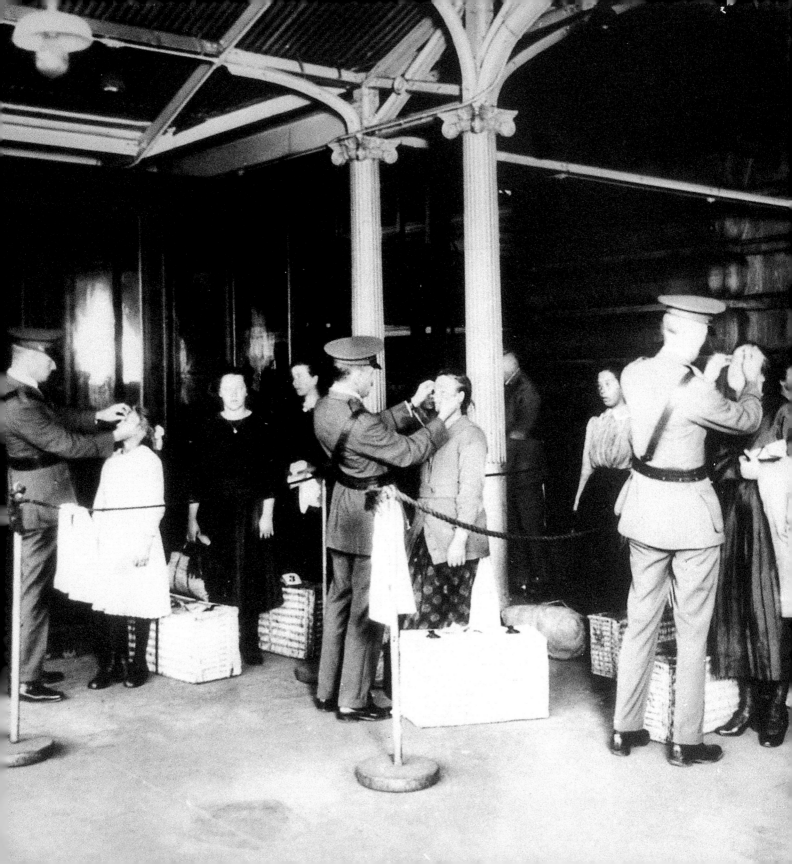

CHAPTER FOUR

The Statue Today— And Beyond

On July 4, 1986, the Statue of Liberty had an early birthday party. Before the celebration could begin, however, the statue had to go through two years of repairs. The *restoration* cost millions of dollars and included replacing the 1,600 rusty iron ribs that hold the statue's copper skin in place with stainless steel ones. The torch was also replaced, and an elevator was installed inside the statue.

◀ *A huge scaffolding surrounds the Statue of Liberty as the repairs begin.*

When the repairs were completed, there were four days of celebrations that included concerts, fireworks, tall ships, and ethnic festivals. Chief Justice Warren E. Burger swore in 5,000 new citizens on Ellis Island, while 20,000 others were *simultaneously* sworn in across the country through a satellite telecast. These ceremonies were followed by others on October 28, the statue's real hundredth birthday.

Did You Know?

The Statue of Liberty has inspired many artists and writers. Emma Lazarus (1849–1887) wrote *The New Colossus* on November 2, 1883. It is a now famous poem that was originally written to raise money to build the statue's pedestal. A bronze plaque bearing the words of the poem was placed on the pedestal in 1903. The closing lines of the poem have become very well known. Do you recognize them?

Give me your tired, your poor,
Your huddled masses yearning to breathe free,
The wretched refuse of your teeming shore;
Send these, the homeless, tempest-tost to me,
I lift my lamp beside the golden door!

Lady Liberty celebrated her hundredth birthday in grand style.

On September 11, 2001, across the water from the Statue of Liberty, a horrible event took place. Two airplanes were taken over by *terrorists* who crashed them into the two towers of the World Trade Center. Both buildings crumbled to the ground, killing thousands of people. Through the horror of the days that followed, the Statue of Liberty stood, tall and proud amid the smoke from the fires of the World Trade Center. It was a true symbol of America's spirit and its people's will to survive. Today the statue and the values it stands for are more important than ever.

◄ *The Statue of Liberty was a symbol of hope to thousands of New Yorkers in the days that followed the collapse of the World Trade Center on September 11, 2001.*

Glossary

courtyard — An open area surrounded by walls.

eternal — Lasting forever.

extend — To make something longer or bigger.

inspire — To fill someone with an emotion, an attitude, or an idea.

pedestal — A base for a statue.

proclaim — To announce publicly.

restoration — To bring back to original condition.

sculptor — An artist who carves or shapes stone, wood, metal, marble, or clay.

simultaneous — Occurring at the same time.

tablet — A piece of stone with writing carved on it.

terrorist — Someone who uses violence or fear as a means of force.

Find Out More

Books

Drummond, Allan. *Liberty!* New York: Farrar, Straus & Giroux, 2002.

Penner, Lucille. *Statue of Liberty*. New York: Random House, 1995.

Quiri, Patricia Ryon. *The Statue of Liberty*. Danbury, CT: Children's Press, 1998.

Web Sites

Statue of Liberty
www.nps.gov/stli

Statue of Liberty Facts
www.endex.com/gf/buildings/liberty/libertyfacts.htm

Statue of Liberty National Monument
www.americanparknetwork.com/parkinfo/sl

Travel Channel
American Icons
Lady Liberty—Symbol of Dreams
http://travel.discovery.com/convergence/americanicon/ladyliberty/statue.html

Index